Mum was checking Kipper's trainers. "Are these your toes at the end?" she asked. "Your feet have grown again!"

"You need a new pair of trainers," said Mum. "Go and tell Biff and Chip that we're going to the shops."

As soon as Kipper peeked into Biff's room, the magic key started to glow.
It was time for an adventure.

The magic took them to a forest with lots of tall trees.

Biff saw a footprint in the mud.

"Look at this," she said. "It's enormous!"

She put her own foot next to the footprint to compare.

"What made it?" asked Kipper. "A bear?"

"Bears have paws with sharp claws," said Biff. "This footprint has toe marks."

"Some people believe a mystery animal called Bigfoot lives in the woods," said Chip.

"Perhaps Bigfoot made the footprint," Chip added.

"Here is another mystery," said Kipper. "Why is this rope here?"

Biff and Chip went to check.

Suddenly a big, wooden cage dropped down over the three children.

"Oh no!" shouted Chip. "It's a trap!"

The children tried to lift up the cage but it was much too heavy.

"Help!" shouted Kipper. "Is anybody there?"

"Yes!" said Biff. "Look over there."
A huge, hairy creature was watching them. It looked interested.

"That's Bigfoot!" said Chip in amazement.
Bigfoot came closer.
"I think he wants to help us," said Biff.

The wooden cage was not heavy for Bigfoot. He lifted it off the children easily. "We're free!" said Chip.

Biff looked up at Bigfoot. "Thanks for helping us," she said.

Bigfoot seemed to smile at the children.

Suddenly they heard gruff voices.

"The trap is this way," said a man.

Bigfoot looked round. Now he seemed frightened.

He ran into the woods and hid.

A moment later three men appeared.

"What are you children doing here?" one of them asked.

"We're lost," said Chip quickly.

"My name is Mr Bunkum," said the man. "We set that trap to catch a mystery animal called Bigfoot."

Bigfoot stayed hidden and watched.
"What will you do if you catch him?"
Biff asked Bunkum.

Bunkum smiled. "I'm going to take him all around the world in my travelling circus. People will pay lots of money to see him. He is the only Bigfoot in the world!"

Bunkum gave the children a hard stare. "Have you seen Bigfoot near here?" he asked.

The children did not think Bunkum's plan sounded very nice for Bigfoot.

Biff, Chip and Kipper looked at each other. They shook their heads.

Chip quietly rubbed his foot over the footprint so the men would not see it.

"Maybe I'll go and look for the Loch Ness monster instead!" Bunkum said crossly.

The magic key began to glow.
"What's that? A magic key!" shouted Bunkum. "People will pay lots to see that!"

The children started disappearing.
"Come back!" Bunkum shouted angrily.
He did not know that Bigfoot was behind him, waving goodbye to the children.

At home Mum was waiting to take Kipper shopping for new trainers.

"Go on then, Bigfoot," joked Biff to her little brother.